Moments Together

for

INTIMACY

DENNIS and BARBARA RAINEY

Regal

From Gospel Light
Ventura, California, U.S.A.

Published by Regal
From Gospel Light
Ventura, California, U.S.A.
www.regalbooks.com
Printed in the U.S.A.

Library of Congress Cataloging-in-Publication Data
Rainey, Dennis, 1948-
[Moments together for couples]
Moments together for intimacy / Dennis and Barbara Rainey.
p. cm.
Originally published: Moments together for couples. Ventura, Calif. :
Regal Books, 1995.
Includes bibliographical references.
ISBN 978-08307-5139-6
1. Spouses—Prayer-books and devotions—English. 2.
Marriage—Religious aspects—Christianity. 3. Devotional calendars. I.
Rainey, Barbara. II. Title.
BV4596.M3 R34 2003
242'.644—dc21
2002156010

6 7 8 9 10 11 12 13 14 / 15 14 13 12 11 10 09

Rights for publishing this book outside the U.S.A. or in non-English languages are administered by Gospel Light Worldwide, an international not-for-profit ministry. For additional information, please visit www.glww.org, email info@glww.org, or write to Gospel Light Worldwide, 1957 Eastman Avenue, Ventura, CA 93003, U.S.A.

INTRODUCTION

Intimacy in marriage. What is it? How do we achieve it?

The word tumbles from the tongue, but do we really understand its meaning? And more important, how do we experience it?

Sex is often thought to mean intimacy, and of course sexual relations in marriage are a part of intimacy. But there's more. Much more.

At its core, to be intimate in marriage is to *know and be known*. Intimacy goes beyond the surface issue of knowing *about* another person to knowing who he or she really is—and being known yourself in the same way. Intimacy involves a lifelong process of knowing and being known *deeply, very deeply*.

Technology has given us the potential to know much about every conceivable topic and even to gather massive amounts of information about another person. But tons of knowledge does not necessarily guarantee one ounce of genuine intimacy in marriage.

True, deep intimacy can only occur in a marriage protected by the most sacred promise a man and woman ever make to another human being: their marriage covenant. Within these secure walls, love and intimacy have a chance to grow. In our culture of divorce, with its shallow view of love, it is no wonder intimacy is so rare in so many marriages. Many modern couples don't even know each other very well, much less find the deep, satisfying currents of intimacy. In the one relationship where intimacy should grow and ripen like luscious fruit in a vineyard, too often the only crops are loneliness, disappointment, pain and regret.

This does not have to be! If you desire greater intimacy in your marriage, we have some advice: Spend more focused time with God and with each other! Intimacy requires more than a lot of relational hanging out. You need to do the right things when you are together to build a relationship that sinks a shaft of unconditional love deep into your souls.

One of the best activities to deepen intimacy is a regular time of joint devotions. Spending some quality time reading Scripture, discussing spiritual topics and praying together will draw you closer. That's why we have created *Moments Together for Intimacy*. This small but practical book will help you create the spiritual environment where your intimacy with God and one another can grow. Here are 30 devotionals, each requiring only about 10 minutes, that will help you and your spouse find deeper intimacy—both with God and each other.

Some of the topics include the following:

> Decision making in marriage
> Communication
> What submission really means
> Understanding differences between men and
>   women
> Truly honoring your wife
> The macho myth
> Why you need romance
> What communicates love

We pray that you and your spouse will seek greater intimacy by using this devotional book to its fullest advantage. If you give it your all, in just 30 days we believe you will *know* each other and God more intimately than ever before.

THE PARABLE OF THE PORCUPINES

For whoever wishes to save his life shall lose it; but whoever loses his life for My sake shall find it.

MATTHEW 16:25

Perhaps you've heard the story of the two porcupines freezing in the winter cold. Shivering in the frigid air, the two porcupines move closer together to share body heat and warmth. But then their sharp spines and quills prick each other painfully and they move apart, victims once more of the bitter cold around them. Soon they again feel they must come together, or they will freeze to death. But their quills cause too much pain and they part again.

Family members suffer from the cold of isolation, too— and they learn of the pain of being close to someone with quills. We desperately need to learn how to live with the barbs that are part of coming together in oneness.

C. S. Lewis describes the urgency of learning this lesson:

Love anything, and your heart will certainly be wrung, possibly be broken. If you want to make sure of keeping it intact, you must give your heart to no one, not even to an animal. Wrap it carefully around with hobbies and little luxuries; avoid all entanglements; lock it up safe in the casket or coffin of your selfishness. But in that casket—safe, dark, motionless, airless—it will change. It will not be broken; it will become unbreakable, impenetrable, irredeemable.[1]

Intimacy extracts a price. The closer I get to Barbara, the more she becomes aware of *who I really am*. The more transparent we become, the greater the possibility that she will reject me. But if both of us are committed to each other despite our quills—if we are willing, as Jesus said, to lose our lives instead of saving them—intimacy awaits us.

Discuss: On a scale of 1 to 5, with 1 at the top of the scale, how would you rate the level of intimacy in your marriage?

Pray: Ask God for openness and intimacy in your family that connects one another's hearts and creates a deep sense of belonging.

Note

1. C. S. Lewis, *The Inspirational Writings of C. S. Lewis* (New York: Inspirational Press, 1994), p. 278.

IF WE ARE WILLING,
AS JESUS SAID, TO LOSE
OUR LIVES INSTEAD OF
SAVING THEM—
INTIMACY AWAITS US.

DAY 2

MOTIVES FOR MARRIAGE

*Many are the plans in a man's heart, but the
counsel of the LORD, it will stand.*

PROVERBS 19:21

Why did you get married? For sex? Romance? Companion-ship? Security? To have children?

There are good reasons for marriage, and there are childish ones. Years ago I read an article in an issue of *McCall's* magazine that included some humorous comments from children:

> Gwen, age 9: "When I get married I want to marry someone who is tall and handsome and rich and hates spinach as much as me."
>
> Arnold, age 6: "I want to get married, but not right away yet because I can't cross the street by myself yet."
>
> Steve, age 10: "I want to marry somebody just like my mother except I hope she don't make me clean up my room."

Bobby, age 9: "I don't have to marry someone who is rich, just someone who gets a bigger allowance than me."

Raymond, age 9: "First she has to like pizza, then she has to like cheesecake, after that she has to like fudge candy, then I know our marriage will last forever."[1]

We chuckle at these childish impressions, yet I have counseled couples whose purposes for getting married were not much more profound. Lucius Annaeus Seneca (4 B.C.-A.D. 65), a Roman philosopher, wrote, "If a man knows not what harbor he seeks, any wind is the right wind."[2]

The book of Genesis describes how, after creating Adam, God realized it was not good for him to be alone, so He gave him a mate.

Since God created marriage, it makes sense that He has a purpose for it. God's blueprint for marriage is the plan to follow, the harbor to which we want to head. In the next few devotionals I will look more closely at His plan for marriage.

Discuss: Why did you marry? What did you hope to get out of marriage?

Pray: Ask that God will spare you and your family from drifting aimlessly through life and that He will give your family His purpose, plan and direction.

Notes
1. *McCall's*. Date and page unknown.
2. "Seneca," *Thinkexist*. www.thinkexist.com/English/Author/
   x/Author_4084 (accessed December 30, 2002).

ƒILLING THE GAPS

*It is not good for the man to be alone; I will
make him a helper suitable for him.*

GENESIS 2:18

God created Adam in a state of isolation in the garden; he
had no human counterpart. So God fashioned a woman to
meet his need for intimacy. In the original text, the Hebrew
word for "helper suitable" means "one matching him."
Adam needed someone who could complement him because
he was inadequate by himself. And this illustrates a third
purpose of marriage: *to complete one another.*

Perhaps you saw the original *Rocky* film before Sylvester
Stallone started spinning off sequels left and right. Do you
remember the love relationship Rocky had with Adrian? She
was the little wallflower who worked in a pet shop, the sister
of Pauly, an insensitive goon who worked at the meat house
and wanted to become a collector of debts for a loan shark.

Pauly couldn't understand why Rocky was attracted to
Adrian. "I don't see it," he said. "What's the attraction?"

Do you remember Rocky's answer? I doubt that the
scriptwriters had any idea what they were saying, but they

perfectly exemplified the principle for a suitable helper from Genesis 2. Rocky said,

> "I don't know; fills gaps, I guess."
> "What's gaps?"
> "She's got gaps. I got gaps. Together we fill gaps."

In his simple but profound way, Rocky hit upon a great truth. He was saying that he and Adrian each had empty places in their lives. But when the two of them got together, they filled those blank spots in one another. And that's exactly what God did when he fashioned a helpmate suitable for Adam. She filled his empty places, and he filled hers.

Have you given much thought to the gaps you fill in your mate's life and vice versa? There's never been any doubt in my mind that I need Barbara, that she fills my gaps. I need her because she tells me the truth about myself, both the good, the bad and otherwise. I need Barbara to add a different perspective to relationships and people. She also adds variety and spice to my life.

Discuss: What gaps do you fill in each other's life?

Pray: Ask that God would give you a thankful heart for these differences.

GOD'S BLUEPRINTS
FOR MARRIAGE
(PART ONE)

And the Lord God fashioned into a woman the rib which He
had taken from the man, and brought her to the man.

GENESIS 2:22

To discover God's plan for marriage, let's return to Genesis 2. As we revisit the Garden of Eden, we watch the drama unfold. God makes Adam but then says, "It isn't good for man to be alone; I will make a companion for him, a helper suited to his needs" (see v. 18). God causes a deep sleep to fall upon Adam. He takes one of his ribs and fashions it into the woman. There is a picture of completeness, and I also believe it's a picture of oneness, because man and woman are made from the same material.

But now we have an all-important question: How would Adam receive Eve? The way many read the familiar Genesis account, Adam's response seems rather ho-hum: "This is now bone of my bones, and flesh of my flesh; she shall be called Woman, because she was taken out of Man" (v. 23). But I like *The Living Bible* paraphrase: "This is it!" In other words, Adam was excited—he was beside himself!

Now, obviously, Eve looked pretty good to Adam. That's why he said, "This is bone of my bones, and flesh of my flesh." She definitely looked better to him than all the animals he had just named, but there is a cornerstone principle for marriage here that we don't want to miss: *Adam had faith in God's integrity.*

Eve had done nothing to earn Adam's response. Adam knew only one thing about Eve—she was a gift from the God he knew intimately. Adam simply accepted her because God made her for him, and he knew that God could be trusted.

Today, God wants us to receive the spouse He has custom-made for us. He can still be trusted.

To reject your mate is to reflect negatively on the character of God. It's as though you are saying, "God, You slipped up, You didn't know what You were doing when You provided this person for me." Rejection of your mate for weakness or for any other reason is disobedience to God and failure to fulfill His plan and purpose for your life.

Will you receive your spouse as God's gift for you?

Discuss: Is there anything about your mate that you don't accept? Are there areas in which you don't feel accepted by your mate?

Pray: Thank God for His gift to you of your spouse.

ADAM KNEW ONLY
ONE THING ABOUT EVE—
SHE WAS A GIFT
FROM THE GOD HE
KNEW INTIMATELY.

GOD'S BLUEPRINTS FOR MARRIAGE

(PART TWO)

For this cause a man shall leave his father and his mother, and shall cleave to his wife; and they shall become one flesh. And the man and his wife were both naked and were not ashamed.

GENESIS 2:24-25

The second part of God's plan for marriage involves construction. You may be noticing a parallel to the Christian life in these blueprints for marriage. First, you receive (accept) Christ and then you build a lifetime of obedient discipleship. After receiving your mate as God's gift (weaknesses and all), you build a lifetime of obedience as husband and wife.

Genesis 2:24 (above) presents four guidelines for building a strong and godly marriage. These are not multiple choice; all four are required for success.

1. *Leave*—that is, establish independence from parents or any others who may have reared you. It's amazing how many people have failed to do this. They may look very adult

and act very mature and sophisticated, but deep down inside they've never really cut the apron strings.

There is a hidden command in this passage to parents: We should let our children leave. A manipulative parent can undermine a marriage whether it's 10 days or 10 years old. We are to let go of our children and let them leave.

2. *Cleave*—that is, form a permanent bond. To cleave means commitment. When God joins two people together, it is for keeps. As the marriage vows say, " 'Til death do us part."

3. *Be physically intimate*—that is, become one flesh in sexual intercourse. Notice the progression: leave, cleave and then one flesh. Physical intimacy comes after the walls of commitment have totally surrounded and secured the relationship.

4. *Become transparent*—that is, be emotionally intimate, totally open and unashamed with your mate. The Genesis account says Adam and Eve were "both naked and were not ashamed." They felt no fear or rejection; instead, they felt total acceptance by each other. Being bathed in the warmth of knowing another person accepts you is what makes marriage a true joy.

Discuss: Evaluate and grade yourselves as a couple on the four guidelines for building a marriage. Where are you winning? Where do you need to work?

Pray: Ask that God would give you success as a couple in each of these four areas of your relationship.

AS THE YEARS GO BY

We love, because He first loved us.
1 JOHN 4:19

I have never hesitated to tell Barbara that I love her. But I remember one time when I was especially surprised by her reply.

We had been married a number of years and perhaps on that day she wanted actions to back up my words, because she said, "Well, I know you love me. But you're supposed to. You're my husband."

At the time, I was puzzled. But she went on to explain that many things test commitment in marriage—and perhaps nothing tests it more than the passage of years. As we mature and go through various seasons of our lives, it's easy to begin wondering if your husband is really just going through the motions by declaring love for you.

Barbara concluded by saying, "When you first marry, you declare your commitment and trust to a person you hardly know."

Isn't that amazing? You *think* you know all about this new life partner, but in reality you probably just see the tip of the iceberg.

As years go by, you see each other in a variety of situations. You see the achievements and the failures. You raise a family, you experience ups and downs in your career, and you struggle through problems with relatives. You develop godly disciplines and, perhaps at the same time, some bad habits. You encounter health problems; you gain weight; your hair turns gray.

And through all that, as your mate grows to know you more than any other person on Earth (and vice versa), it's easy to begin thinking, *I know you say you're committed to me, but are you* glad *you are committed to me? Would you do this again? You say you love me, but do you* really?

Many marriages fail because both partners lose their commitment and trust over the years. No matter what struggles you work through, no matter how many heated discussions you have until 2:00 A.M., each of you should know without a shadow of doubt that you have no escape clause in your marriage vows.

And in the end, your commitment needs to be based on one thing: your faith in the God who brought you together. That bedrock should be like a granite foundation—rock solid and immovable.

Discuss: What has tested your marriage commitment over the years?

Pray: Ask that God would deepen your relationship with Him and, therefore, deepen your commitment to each other.

YOUR COMMITMENT
TO EACH OTHER NEEDS
TO BE BASED ON ONE THING:
YOUR FAITH IN THE
GOD WHO BROUGHT
YOU TOGETHER.

WIVES WERE MEANT TO SOAR

*For in this way in former times the holy women
also, who hoped in God, used to adorn themselves,
being submissive to their own husbands.*

1 PETER 3:5

There is a story about a kite that was soaring high in the sky when it saw a field of flowers some distance away. *It sure would be fun to fly over there and get a closer look at all those beautiful flowers,* the kite thought.

But there was one problem. The string holding the kite wasn't long enough to let it fly where it wanted to, so it pulled and tugged and finally broke loose. Happily, the kite soared for a few moments toward the field of flowers. But soon it came crashing down—falling far short of its goal. What had seemed to be holding the kite down was actually enabling it to fly.

The wife is the kite in this story. The string symbolizes the scriptural principles of a man's responsibility to lead and of a woman's responsibility to submit to his headship. The string was not intended to be a hindrance. Together with the wind, it is actually what is holding up the kite.

The husband's love is the wind that enables the kite to soar into the sky. Without this wind—the secure, encouraging environment the husband creates through his leadership—the wife can feel tied down, not uplifted.

A husband can help his wife soar by reminding her verbally of his love and expressing his need of her in specific ways—notes, calls and love letters. And he can show appreciation to her for all that she does for him.

Husbands need to give the kind of servant-based leadership that uplifts their wives. God means for this leadership to be liberating, not limiting. God made wives to soar.

Discuss: As a wife, share with your husband ways he could enable you to soar. What are three things he can do to add lift to your life?

Pray: As a husband, take your wife's hand and express to God how grateful you are for her.

GOD MEANS FOR A
HUSBAND'S LEADERSHIP
TO BE LIBERATING,
NOT LIMITING.

DECISION MAKING IN MARRIAGE

But I want you to understand that Christ is the head of every man, and the man is the head of a woman, and God is the head of Christ. However, in the Lord, neither is woman independent of man, nor is man independent of woman.

1 CORINTHIANS 11:3,11

Barbara and I made a commitment early in our marriage that we would make all decisions together. Only if we come to an honest yet unshakable disagreement do I make the decision as head of the house.

I mention this because many men use their headship as a sort of club to force their wives to submit. I don't think it's a mistake that Paul writes, "Neither is woman independent of man, nor is man independent of woman." We need each other in marriage—and in the decisions we make as a couple.

One lesson I've learned with decision making in our marriage is that just because Barbara says something once doesn't mean that she's felt like I have heard her. Sometimes I need to hear her again and again and understand the emotional power behind her words. This is especially important when she disagrees with a decision I make because only if she knows I understand her, will she be ready to follow that decision.

In a decision we made about our daughter Rebecca's gymnastics involvement, I maintained that we should move her out of gymnastics. As Barbara recalls, "I knew intuitively Dennis was probably right, but I wasn't ready to make that decision yet. I loved watching Rebecca perform. She was built for gymnastics and she loved it.

"I also was concerned because I didn't want her to grow up and resent us for forcing her to quit. I needed to share with Dennis how I felt. It just took me time to come to where I felt like I had adequately expressed that."

The reality was, there was truth in what Barbara said. Her cautions against Rebecca resenting that decision were sound. As husbands we err in decision making when we don't really take our wife's opinion into account. It is the wise man who does!

Discuss: What do you like most about the way you and your mate make decisions? Least?

Pray: Is there a decision you need to make? Why not stop and pray together about that decision right now?

WHAT DOES SUBMISSION REALLY MEAN?

BY BARBARA RAINEY

In the same way, you wives, be submissive
to your own husbands.

1 PETER 3:1

There is no doubt that a wife's submission is one of the most controversial concepts in the Bible. Just mention the word and many women immediately become angry and even hostile. This subject of submission has been highly debated and misunderstood.

The dictionary doesn't help because one definition of "submissive" is "unresistingly or humbly obedient."[1]

Who wants to be described like that? I certainly don't. Negative definitions of "submission" often lead to abuses of the concept by husbands who fail to understand its biblical meaning and the man's role in a marriage.

Some husbands and wives actually believe submission indicates that women are inferior to men or that women have no right to challenge something their husbands say or do. Submitting doesn't mean that you tolerate abuse or neglect.

It does mean respecting your husband and allowing him to lead in your relationship. It means interacting with your husband on every key decision, sharing your perspective as his partner and then trusting your husband. It means being supportive in what he does right.

My husband needs my *voluntary* submission in order to become the servant-leader God wants him to be. And when Dennis loves me the way he is commanded to, it is easier for me to submit to him and his leadership.

Discuss: In what ways, as a woman, are you thankful for your husband's leadership?

Pray: Pray that submission and authority will not be a problem in your home.

Note
1. *Random House Unabridged Dictionary*, 2nd ed., s.v. "submissive."

My husband needs
my *voluntary* submission
in order to become
the servant-leader God
wants him to be.

RESPECTING
A RESPECTFUL
HUSBAND

BY BARBARA RAINEY

*Nevertheless let each individual among you also
love his own wife even as himself; and let the wife
see to it that she respect her husband.*

EPHESIANS 5:33

Unfortunately, some men hear only Paul's words about women being submissive and take this as license to be domineering. It's impossible for a wife to submit to a man who doesn't respect her needs as a woman.

Every husband needs a wife who respects him. That means she notices him, regards him, honors him, prefers him and esteems him. From a negative point of view, not respecting your husband means to be insulting, critical, nonsupportive or passive towards him and his needs.

One way to respect your husband is to consider and understand the weight of his responsibilities as a servant-leader in the home. It is easy to look at your husband and see what is wrong instead of right. As someone once said,

"Faults are like the headlights of your car—those of others seem more glaring."

Your husband needs unconditional acceptance—faults and all. As a Kenny Rogers song puts it:

> She believes in me.
> I'll never know just what she sees in me . . .
> But she believes in me.[1]

One way to communicate respect to your husband is to accept his schedule. For example, in past years I had to learn to be content with a schedule that found us packing up and leaving for most of the summer for Dennis's teaching assignments, conferences and meetings. We also had to learn how to live a great deal of time out of a suitcase and even out of the car.

When it gets to be too much, I tell Dennis and we make adjustments. Yes, my husband's schedule is important to me. I choose to be a part of what he does, to watch and help, and to be available to him. And I know by choosing to support Dennis in these ways, I am actually showing him respect.

Discuss: Ask your husband when he has most felt respected by you. Ask him why.

Pray: As a wife, ask God to grant you a better understanding of your husband's needs so that you will be able to know how to express your respect for him.

Note
1. Steve Gibb, "She Believes in Me," on record 4 of *20 Great Years*, Kenny Rogers, Reprise, 1990.

EVERY HUSBAND NEEDS
A WIFE WHO NOTICES HIM,
REGARDS HIM, HONORS HIM,
PREFERS HIM AND
ESTEEMS HIM.

A FELLOW HEIR

*And grant her honor as a fellow
heir of the grace of life.*

1 PETER 3:7

Today the business world has all kinds of partnerships: silent partners, financial partners, equal partners, controlling partners, minority partners, and more. But in marriage, God intended for us to have only one kind: a fully participating partnership.

The apostle Peter sets forth the concept of mutual partnership as he instructs a man to treat his wife as "a fellow heir of the grace of life." Although her function and role as a woman differ from yours as a man, she has an equal inheritance as a child of God.

You will make your wife a participating partner in your life when you tenderly look her in the eyes and say "I need you." Why not make this an experiential reality in your marriage by frequently saying:

- "I need you to listen as I talk about what's troubling me. And I need your perspective on my problems and your belief in me as a person."
- "I need you to help me become the man God created me to be."

- "I want you to have total access into my life. I need you to keep me honest in areas of my life in which I could stray from Christ. You may question me or confront me on any issue."
- "You are the person I most trust with my life."
- "I need you for your advice, judgments and wise counsel on decisions I face, especially at work."
- "I need your prayers for a temptation I am facing."

When I become the sole proprietor in our marriage and treat Barbara as a silent partner, we both lose. She loses the opportunities I can give to include her, develop her and make her feel important. And I lose because I tend to make poor decisions when I am isolated from her.

Most wives beam with joy when their husbands let them into the interior of their lives. Wives long to be trusted with their husbands' challenges, emotions and self-doubts.

Discuss: Discuss this concept of partnership. Does your wife feel she is part of your life? What adjustments can you make to make her your partner?

Pray: Ask that God would give you the courage as a man to give your wife even greater access to your life and that He would use you as a team to be more effective than you would be as individuals.

GRANT HER HONOR
AS A FELLOW HEIR
OF THE GRACE OF LIFE.

1 PETER 3:7

GIVE YOURSELF UP

*Husbands, love your wives, just as Christ also loved the
church and gave Himself up for her.*

EPHESIANS 5:25

We all realize that well-known pastors and Christian leaders are as human as anyone else, yet something within us
always remains surprised when we hear them tell stories that
demonstrate just how fallible they are!

That was the case when I interviewed pastor and author
Chuck Swindoll for a *FamilyLife Today* broadcast. Chuck was
talking about a key event in his relationship with his wife,
Cynthia: The day he realized how selfish he was.

They had been married for 10 years and were sitting in
their kitchen in Boston. Cynthia began crying and said,
"Honey, I don't want you to tell people that we are partners
in ministry anymore. Because we're not."

Chuck was stunned. "What do you mean?" he asked.

"You don't really want me as a partner," she replied.
"You just kind of need me at certain times. I'm not the Holy
Spirit in your life, and I'm not giving you an agenda. I can
just tell you I am one unhappy woman. I feel distant from
the ministry. When I hear you preach, I'm watching one

man. When I live with you, I'm with another."

As Chuck looks back on that day, he sees it as a turning point in his marriage. "I really was living a single life as a married man," he recalls. "When I saw it, I was ashamed. That's the only word I know to use.

"I began to see little things I had done for 10 years, such as not bothering to introduce Cynthia to others. When she served the meat, I'd take the biggest piece. I'd tell jokes about her. If we had a busy weekend, I'd take care of my agenda. She'd take up the slack.

"I realized I am a selfish man."

Since then Chuck and Cynthia began forging a true partnership in their ministry; in fact, he says his best ideas come from her. Their marriage stands as a testimony to the grace of God because Chuck is living out the truth of Ephesians 5:25 by "giving himself up" for his beloved Cynthia.

Discuss: How do you treat your wife? Would she say you are unselfish?

Pray: Ask God to help you be the servant-leader your wife needs you to be.

TENDERLY LOOK
HER IN THE EYES AND
SAY "I NEED YOU."

ARE YOU LISTENING?

Be gracious to me, O God, according to Thy lovingkindness;
according to the greatness of Thy compassion blot out my
transgressions. Wash me thoroughly from my iniquity,
and cleanse me from my sin.

PSALM 51:1-2

King David had sent a man to his death, so he could take that man's wife for his own. When the prophet Nathan rebuked him for this terrible sin, David had a choice: He could turn from God (perhaps even finding a way to blame others for what he had done), or he could admit his offense and repent.

As we all know, David recognized that God was speaking to him through Nathan, and he decided to repent. The beautiful words of Psalm 51 speak of his broken heart.

I wonder how many people hear God speaking through another person and yet make the wrong choice? What if Chuck Swindoll, in that defining moment in his kitchen during his tenth year of marriage, had refused to listen to his wife's cry of pain? What if he had continued in his selfish ways?

One of two things probably would have occurred: (1) he might have continued to progress and achieve fame and notoriety—only to have his life and ministry fall apart at a later date; or (2) God might have clamped shut the working of the Holy Spirit in and through him, and today he'd be ministering somewhere with very little impact.

Sooner or later, a man who continues on the path of selfishness and rebellion will end up empty and defeated. If he is fortunate, he will listen to the voice of the Holy Spirit, often speaking through his mate, early on and save himself years of misery.

When Cynthia Swindoll told Chuck that she didn't feel part of his ministry, "It was like a light clicked on in the room." He told himself, *Swindoll, wake up. This is the best thing you could be hearing. This could be the making of your marriage.*

You can thrive in a marriage when you commit to create a partnership under the guidance of the Holy Spirit—and when you're willing to listen to Him speaking.

Discuss: What has God taught you through your mate? In what situations has the Holy Spirit used your mate to help you become more Christlike?

Pray: Take your wife's hand and genuinely thank God for her.

TAKE YOUR WIFE'S HAND
AND GENUINELY THANK
GOD FOR HER.

UNDERSTANDING SEXUAL DIFFERENCES

I am my beloved's, and his desire is for me.

SONG OF SOLOMON 7:10

𝒜 TV talk-show host was interviewing one of Hollywood's biggest male stars, a man known for his prowess with the opposite sex. At one point, the host asked him what it takes to be a great lover.

The actor replied with two criteria: A great lover is a man who can satisfy one woman over a lifetime; and it is a man who can be satisfied with one woman for a lifetime. I wanted to shout "Amen!"

Husband and wife must be committed to satisfying one another's physical and emotional needs. But they also must both take it upon themselves to understand each other's differing needs and attitudes about sexuality.

A frequent problem is that husbands expect their wives to be just as interested in sex as they are. In a survey in Tallahassee, Florida, 230 married couples were given a list of 96 possible leisure activities and asked to pick the 5 they enjoyed the most. The list included watching TV, gardening, going to church, visiting friends, sex, athletic events, reading and sewing. Among the men, 45 percent picked "Engaging in sexual or affectionate activities" as their first choice. Among the women, 37 percent ranked reading first, with sex barely edging out sewing for pleasure!

Most men want physical oneness, while women desire emotional oneness. The man is stimulated by sight, smell and the body; the woman is stimulated by touch, attitudes, actions, words—the whole person.

A man needs respect and admiration, to be physically needed and not to be put down. The woman needs understanding, love, to be emotionally needed and time to warm up to sexual intimacy.

As you understand your mate's needs, you can sacrificially act to meet them in loving, caring ways.

Discuss: How can you communicate to your mate that he or she is important to you sexually? What differences have you discovered between the two of you in this area?

Pray: Ask God to help you and your mate understand one another and develop an intimate knowledge of each other—emotionally, spiritually and physically.

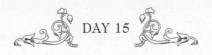

THE "ONE FLESH" CHALLENGE

BY BARBARA RAINEY

And the two shall become one flesh.

EPHESIANS 5:31

As a wife, I believe the Bible calls me to commit to my husband in a mutually fulfilling sexual relationship— truly to become "one flesh" with my husband. That means I need to understand his needs and desires in this area.

My husband's sexual needs should be more important and higher on my priority list than menus, housework, projects, activities—even the children. A friend shared something with me that I think puts the sexual dimension of a man in a biblical perspective. A man can send his clothes to the laundry, eat all of his meals out, find companionship with friends, be accepted and respected at work, and be listened to by a counselor and in all those things not go against the will of God. But if he meets his sexual needs with someone other than his wife, it is sin.

I believe that many wives don't really understand how important the act of "becoming one" is to our husbands. We make time for the PTA, church work and helping a child with homework. Think about it: How often do you set aside time to be together? It may be a weekend getaway or a romantic dinner in your bedroom.

Perhaps one of the most spiritual acts a wife might need to do is put the kids to bed and invite her husband to go to bed early.

Discuss: At an appropriate time, ask your husband to share his needs in this area. You might want to share what would create sexual fulfillment in your marriage.

Pray: Ask God to help you both better understand one another's needs and how you can act to meet them on a regular basis.

HONORING YOUR WIFE

A gracious woman attains honor.

PROVERBS 11:16

After watching the marriages of numerous Christian leaders disintegrate, I have come to some conclusions. One is that there is no such thing as a marriage blowout—only slow, small leaks. Like a tire that gradually loses air without the driver noticing, these marriages were allowed to slowly go flat. If one of the spouses had checked the air pressure in the marriage, he or she certainly hadn't done anything to return it to an acceptable, safe level.

Every marriage is susceptible to leaks, and ours is no exception. The world lures my wife with glittery, false promises of fulfillment and true significance. If I fail to honor her and esteem her as a woman of distinction, it's just a matter of time before she will begin to wear down and look elsewhere for worth.

How can you honor your wife? I'll share with you a few techniques.

Learn the art of putting her on a pedestal. Capture your wife's heart by treating her with respect, tenderness and the highest esteem.

Recognize her accomplishments. Frequently I look into Barbara's eyes and verbally express my wonder at all she does. She wears many hats and is an amazingly hard worker. At other times, I stand back in awe of the woman of character she has become. Her steady walk with God is a constant stream of ministry to me.

Speak to her with respect. Without careful attention, your tongue can become caustic, searing and accusing. I work hard to honor Barbara. I'm not always as successful as I'd like to be, but I know that honor begins with an attitude. Also, when the kids were young, if they ever talked back to Barbara or showed disrespect, they knew they would have to deal with me when I got home. Our children are great, but they would have mugged her if I let them. She's outnumbered! So I still encourage our children to respect her.

Honor your wife by extending common courtesies. You may think that these little amenities were worthwhile only during courtship, but actually they are great ways to demonstrate respect and distinction over the long haul. Common courtesy is at the heart of servanthood; it says "my life for yours." It bows before another to show esteem and dignity.

Why not increase the air pressure in your marriage today by honoring your wife?

Discuss: Discuss the air pressure in your marriage tire—any leaks? A patch needed? What are two ways you can honor your wife this week?

Pray: Ask that you would discern slow leaks in your marriage before they cause serious problems and that your wife would feel honored in her critical roles as wife and mother.

THERE IS NO SUCH THING
AS A MARRIAGE BLOWOUT—
ONLY SLOW, SMALL LEAKS.

THE MACHO MYTH

BY BARBARA RAINEY

This is my beloved and this is my friend.
SONG OF SOLOMON 5:16

One day Dennis gave me a list of what he considered to be the needs most men have:

- Self-confidence in his manhood
- To be listened to
- Companionship
- To be needed sexually by his wife
- To be accepted and respected

Counselors and pastors would give you similar lists based on their experiences. And you know what this tells me? The macho man—self-contained, independent and invulnerable—is a myth.

To bolster Dennis's confidence, I try to encourage him by being his best friend. Every husband wants his wife to be on his team, to coach him when necessary but most of all to be his cheerleader. A husband needs a wife who is behind him, believing in him, appreciating him and cheering him on as he goes out into the world every day.

The word "appreciate" means to "raise in value."[1] When I give Dennis words of praise and encouragement, I raise his value, not only in his eyes, but in mine as well; and that builds his confidence as a man.

The psychologist William James said, "The deepest principle of human nature is the craving to be appreciated." And Charles Swindoll said, "We live by encouragement and die without it—slowly, sadly and angrily."[2]

When is the last time you told your husband you appreciated him?

Discuss: As a husband, share with your wife the times you have felt most appreciated by her. As a wife, ask your husband how you can be his cheerleader.

Pray: As a wife, take your husband's hand and express to God your appreciation for him.

Notes
1. *Webster's New College Dictionary*, 2nd ed., s.v. "appreciate."
2. Sources of quotes unknown.

EVERY HUSBAND
WANTS HIS WIFE TO BE
ON HIS TEAM AND TO BE
HIS CHEERLEADER.

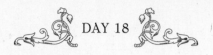
THE MUTUAL ADMIRATION SOCIETY

BY BARBARA RAINEY

How delightful is a timely word!

PROVERBS 15:23

During the early months of our marriage, Dennis and I spontaneously complimented and praised each other for newly discovered characteristics. It became almost a game to see who could find another good quality to praise. We named our exclusive club the Mutual Admiration Society.

When our house became full of children, the situation was not quite the same, but the Mutual Admiration Society still convened. Some evenings at the dinner table we raised a question such as, What do you appreciate most about Dad? Then we each in turn around the table answered the question. We heard such classic comments as, "He goes fishing with me"; "He goes on dates with me"; and from our daughter Rebecca when she was just five, "He sneaks chocolate with me." It was very difficult to be depressed when a chorus of youngsters was cheering you on.

William James said, "All of us, in the glow of feeling we have pleased, want to do more to please." Thus, you can help to motivate your mate toward excellence in his or her character and his or her performance by giving generous, liberal and fervent praise.

Don't forget to praise your mate for those mundane daily duties. Make a mental note of those unpleasant, difficult tasks, and give a verbal reward of encouragement the next time he or she completes one. Anytime Dennis fixes something around the house, for example, I am quick to express my appreciation. I know how inept he feels in this area and what it takes for him to crank up the courage at least to try!

Your mate also needs you to praise him or her specifically for who he or she is as a person. Sow the good seeds of praise in his or her life with positive, encouraging statements:

"I appreciate you because you . . ."
"I admire you for your . . ."
"Thank you for . . ."

You can watch your mate's encouragement value go up when you appreciate him or her verbally!

Discuss: List three things your mate has done lately that are deserving of praise. Write them in a love note to him or her.

Pray: Ask that God will develop within you the determination to build your relationship by praising each other.

MOTIVATE YOUR MATE
TOWARD EXCELLENCE IN HIS
OR HER CHARACTER BY
GIVING GENEROUS, LIBERAL
AND FERVENT PRAISE.

A WOMAN'S EMOTIONS
(PART ONE)
BY BARBARA RAINEY

Do not let the sun go down while you are still angry.

EPHESIANS 4:26 (*NIV*)

We know we are created in the image of God, but many of us don't realize our *emotions* are a part of God's image imprinted within us. Women need to grow in their understanding of their emotions. And this isn't easy, because many women aren't prepared to handle the different emotions they feel at different stages of their lives.

As a woman experiences various emotions, she needs to feel loved and accepted, so she can face these times positively. This is not only critical for her emotional health but also for impacting her children with positive emotional identities, so they will grow up to be mature adults. These emotions are a part of the image of God, and we should grow and mature when we experience them.

When we got married, Dennis and I were completely caught off guard by my emotions as we moved into a marriage relationship. I remember the first time I was angry with Dennis. I had never felt angry with him during the entire time we dated, during our engagement or in the early days of our marriage. I honestly didn't know what to do about my anger.

I remember thinking, *What do I do? Where do I go?* Dennis was pursuing me to solve our conflict, and I was so confused that I went into the bathroom, shut the door and thought, *I can't get out of here. I'm stuck.* My emotions were telling me something was very wrong in this relationship.

I held the future of my marriage and my family in my hands. I decided that my relationship, which was a covenant I'd made to God, was too important not to work it out. So after stewing for a while, I got up out of that bathroom and Dennis and I, after some real communication, resolved the problem.

Dennis and I have found that God designed marriage as a covenant relationship in which a man and woman can work through their emotions and glorify God in the process.

Discuss: How are you in controlling your emotions when it comes to dealing with your mate or your children?

Pray: Ask the Holy Spirit to fill you, guide you and direct you in how you are to handle your emotions in your marriage and family relationships.

A Woman's Emotions
(Part Two)

Let everyone be quick to hear,
slow to speak and slow to anger.

JAMES 1:19

There is this maddening part of being a man. When Barbara comes to me with a problem, my mind immediately shifts into a "fix it" mode. I want to solve the problem—you know: get to the bottom line! But often, the most important thing our wives need is to know we hear them and we care.

One day Barbara came to me discouraged because our lives had been incredibly busy, and she hadn't been at home as much as she wanted. She had been so busy going to ministry, church and school activities and driving kids to different functions, that she had been unable to clean the house.

And guess how I handled it. First, I took it personally. I said, "Well, I help around the house a lot." But she wasn't accusing me of not helping—she was just sharing a burden she felt.

Then, as was typical, I came up with a solution. That night, I declared, the entire family would participate in a

Clean Up the House campaign. And once again I missed the real issue—how she felt. It took a few moments for me to understand that what she needed was for me to just listen and understand her.

So I dug myself out of the hole I'd fallen into and told Barbara I was sorry I had missed her clues, that I didn't hear what she needed. I began to move toward her with the understanding and compassion she needed in the first place.

Want some advice? When your wife approaches you with a problem, repeat back to her what you think she said and ask her to confirm it. For example, I could have said to Barbara, "It sounds to me like you're discouraged because you feel like you've been busy. And the kids and I have allowed the house to get to where it looks like a small volcano has gone off. Is that right?"

Believe it or not, men, often that's all a wife needs—an understanding husband. Resist the urge to fix it immediately.

Discuss: Ask your wife if this is what she generally needs in the above situation.

Pray: Ask that God will give you the ability to live with your wife "in an understanding way" (1 Peter 3:7). Ask Him to help you communicate this to your wife.

OFTEN THE MOST
IMPORTANT THING OUR
WIVES NEED IS TO KNOW
WE HEAR THEM AND
WE CARE.

WHY YOU NEED ROMANCE

[Love] flashes fire, the very flame of Jehovah.
Many waters cannot quench the flame of love,
neither can the floods drown it.

SONG OF SOLOMON 8:6-7 (TLB)

There's a cynical one-liner that goes "The period of engagement is like an exciting introduction to a dull book." Unfortunately, this is true for many couples.

What is it about marriage that seems to dull our romantic creativity? At some point in almost every marriage, a couple realizes that they just don't experience the same romantic feelings they once enjoyed.

Romance is not the foundation of a marriage. But it is the fire in the fireplace—the warmth and security of a relationship that says "We may have struggles, but I love you and everything is okay."

We need that fire in our marriages because we are emotional beings. While we cannot base marriage on romantic feelings, we also can't deny our needs for closeness and intimacy. Without these qualities in a relationship, a couple will drift into isolation.

Barbara and I have had some great romantic highlights in our years together: a fall foliage trip to New England on our tenth anniversary, a getaway at a cozy bed-and-breakfast, candlelight dinners at home after the kids were in bed (when they were young) . . . I could go on and on.

For us, adventure has always spelled romance. And I wasn't surprised one time when I asked Barbara, "Out of all the adventures and romantic times we've had together, what has been your favorite?"

Her answer: "Our honeymoon." For us it was an all-time memory maker. I won't bore you with the details, but I took weeks to plan a two-week honeymoon in the Colorado Rockies. We went camping (and, to our surprise, got some snow) and stayed in a cabin next to a roaring river.

She loved our time together because it was an adventure with plenty of time for just the two of us to talk and share our thoughts and our dreams.

I'll wager that your marriage could use more romance.

Discuss: As you look back on your time together, what have been the romantic highlights? Do you think you have lost some of that romantic fire you once had? What can you do to fan the embers?

Pray: Ask God to equip you to be the romantic partner your spouse needs you to be.

ROMANCE IS NOT
THE FOUNDATION OF A
MARRIAGE, BUT IT IS THE FIRE
IN THE FIREPLACE.

WHAT COMMUNICATES LOVE TO WOMEN

(PART ONE)

So husbands ought also to love their own wives as their own bodies. . . . for no one ever hated his own flesh, but nourishes and cherishes it, just as Christ also does the church.

EPHESIANS 5:28-29

What would your wife do if you looked her in the eye one night and asked, "Sweetheart, what can I do to let you know that I love you? What communicates love to you?"

I know from experience that many wives would respond in one of several ways:

- Fall to the floor in shock, stunned that her husband would even ask
- Run to the bathroom and return with a thermometer, certain that he must not be feeling well
- Laugh cynically and change the subject, figuring that he's probably just joking
- Frown with suspicion, knowing from experience that her husband is just trying to manipulate her, so he can get something he wants

I wish that didn't sound so cynical, but many men seem to lose their romantic ardor once they marry. Some men stop thinking of what communicates love to their wives and focus on trying to meet their own needs.

If you ask this question of your wife, she may not have an answer immediately. She probably hasn't had time to think about it. But she will be pleased you are interested in meeting her needs.

Once you learn the answer, you will need to follow through and demonstrate your love to her with no strings attached. Too often, as men, we think of romance as a means to an end—and that end is sex. We think, *If I do this for my wife, she'll really be responsive in bed tonight!*

If that's your attitude, your wife will sense it quickly. That's not sacrificial love. When you seek to please your wife in this area of romance, you've got to understand you need to deny your agenda and let the goal be solely to help her feel loved, nourished and cherished.

Discuss: Ask your wife what makes her feel loved. Now c'mon, think about this one for a while. This could be really fun and educational!

Pray: Ask that you would be able to nourish and cherish your wife with no strings attached and no agenda of your own to fulfill.

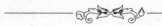

ASK YOUR WIFE WHAT MAKES HER FEEL LOVED.

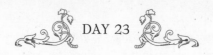

WHAT COMMUNICATES LOVE TO WOMEN
(PART TWO)
BY BARBARA RAINEY

My beloved is mine, and I am his.

SONG OF SOLOMON 2:16

As Dennis wrote in the last devotional, the best way to learn what says "I love you" to your wife is to ask her. But to give you a little more help, we surveyed 800 people at our FamilyLife Marriage Conferences. Here is half of our top 10 list, in reverse order, of what communicates romantic love to women:

10. *Holding hands.* To a woman, this simple act communicates closeness. It says "I want to be close to you and I like you."

9. *Massage.* Many woman are reluctant to ask their husbands for foot rubs or back rubs because they know that most men tend to see massage as sexual foreplay. But women often enjoy massages with no strings attached.

8. *Acts of servanthood and sacrifice.* Sometimes it's as simple as opening the door for your wife or cleaning the dishes after dinner. When a husband denies himself, even in little ways, he tells her he cares about her and he wants to make her feel special.

7. *A kiss.* It's interesting that men ranked this higher than women. I suspect women would rank kissing higher if they didn't know from experience that their husbands usually don't want to stop with a kiss.

6. *Taking a walk together.* Again, this is not usually high on men's lists. It's very relational. When you go for a walk with your husband, you are taking a break from daily responsibilities and distractions. You're away from the telephone and the television, away from children, away from work. It allows you to focus on the relationship in a nonthreatening way.

After looking at this part of the list, I was struck with how God has made women different from one another. And how, as a woman, different things communicate romantic love to me at different times. But we all have one thing in common: We want to feel that our husbands love us.

Discuss: Look over this devotion with your wife and ask her, "Which of these items most communicates love to you?"

Pray: Ask that God would develop within you the desire to communicate love to your wife without any expectation of her response.

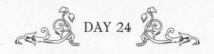

WHAT COMMUNICATES LOVE TO WOMEN

(PART THREE)
BY BARBARA RAINEY

How much better is your love than wine.
SONG OF SOLOMON 4:10

*H*ere is the other half of our top 10 list of what communicates romantic love to women:

5. *Written notes, letters or cards.* Recently, I was cleaning our bathroom and I found an old note from Dennis: "Have you found all your little notes around that say how much I love you?" He had once left notes like this all around the house, and I had a great time searching for them. I had taped this one on a closet wall in the bathroom just to remind me of my wonderful husband.

4. *Going out on a date.* Again, a date means time away, with no kids, just the two of you. A wife likes to be the focus of her husband's attention. She enjoys having a block of time where she has him all to herself.

3. *Having special meals together.* You can put the kids to bed a little early and have a quiet candlelight dinner at home. You can pick up your wife at her office at noon and take her for a short picnic.

2. *Touch.* I'm not talking about sexual touch here but hugging, cuddling, caressing without expectation of a later payoff. Many women never received much physical affection from their parents, so they grew up with a longing for physical touch; if all they get from their husbands is touch that is tied to sex, they will begin thinking, *He really doesn't love me that much. He just needs me for his own pleasure.*

1. *Flowers.* Many men never understand the power of flowers on women, and I'm not sure if I understand it myself. I think flowers say "You are special." I think perhaps it's because flowers are so frivolous—they will wilt and die in a few days, but for that brief period of time you see a constant bright reminder that your husband loves you.

You'll note that a few themes run through this list: Women want to feel special. They want you to show love without an expectation of sex. For women,

romance = relationship.

Discuss: Again, look through this list and ask your wife which items most communicate love to her. Talk about the equation: romance = relationship. Agree or disagree?

Pray: Ask that God will enable you to keep romance alive in your marriage.

WOMEN WANT TO
FEEL SPECIAL.

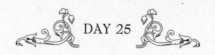

Avoiding Emotional Adultery

Now to Him who is able to keep you from
stumbling, and to make you stand in the presence
of His glory blameless with great joy.

JUDE 24

It is far easier to commit emotional adultery than you may realize. You may be converging on a chemical reaction with another person when:

- You've got a need you feel your mate isn't meeting—a need for attention, approval or affection, for example.
- You find it easier to unwind with someone other than your spouse by dissecting the day's difficulties over lunch, coffee or a ride home.
- You begin to talk about problems you are having with your spouse.
- You rationalize the propriety of this relationship with the opposite sex by saying that surely it must be God's will to talk so openly and honestly with a fellow Christian.

- You look forward to being with this person more than with your own mate.
- You hide the relationship from your mate.

When you find yourself connecting with another person as a substitute for your spouse, you've started traveling a road that ends too often in adultery and divorce. But how do you protect yourself to keep this from occurring?

Know your boundaries. You should put fences around your heart that protect sacred ground, reserved only for your spouse. Barbara and I are careful to share our deepest feelings, needs and difficulties with each other and not with friends of the opposite sex.

Realize the power of your eyes. As has been said, your eyes are the windows to your heart. Pull the shades down if you sense someone is pausing a little too long in front of your windows.

Beware of isolation and concealment. One strategy of the enemy is to isolate you from your spouse, especially by inducing you to keep secrets from your mate.

Extinguish chemical reactions that have already begun. A friendship with the opposite sex that meets the needs your mate should be meeting must be ended quickly. It may be a painful loss at first, but it isn't as painful as dealing with the wreckage caused by a sinful relationship.

Discuss: What barriers can you observe to avoid dangerous chemical reactions?

Pray: Ask daily that God would "keep you from stumbling."

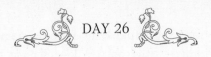

ENTERING THE ATTIC

Brethren, I do not regard myself as having laid hold
of it yet; but one thing I do: forgetting what lies behind
and reaching forward to what lies ahead.

PHILIPPIANS 3:13

Did you know a husband and wife can help each other sort through the attic of the past?

Sue and Rich dated and fell in love during college. Soon they were engaged and then married. Although Sue had shared many things openly as they dated, Rich had no idea how the lack of her father's unconditional approval had shaped her self-image and influenced her life.

When Sue was a young girl, her militaristic father inspected her bedroom every Friday evening. In preparation, she would balance one chair on another to dust the tops of the window and door facings, which her father routinely examined.

All other required work was scrutinized just as intently. Once she was grounded for two weeks for missing two sprigs of crabgrass when she weeded the lawn.

When Sue was 11, she was told to take two cases of soft drinks down the basement stairs. She could barely manage to pick them up, but she did. Halfway down, she tripped and fell head over heels to the concrete floor. She was lying in the midst of broken glass when her father jerked her up and, without inquiring about her well-being, said, "You dummy! I told you not to drop them!"

Not surprisingly, Sue had an impoverished self-image. At times during her marriage, her insecurity surfaced in the form of emotional withdrawal. Rich was often caught off guard, but he encouraged her to tell him about her experiences. He rarely said, "You shouldn't feel that way."

He remained committed to helping her resolve and not repress her feelings about her parents. As a result, Sue now feels loved and valued by God and Rich. She is learning to forget what lies behind and to reach for what is ahead.

Discuss: How familiar are you with your mate's relationship with his or her parents? If you haven't ever done so, take an evening and have your mate share his or her most memorable times with his or her parents.

Pray: Ask that you and your mate will have intimacy to share both positive and negative aspects of the baggage from childhood.

HELP EACH OTHER
LEARN TO FORGET WHAT
LIES BEHIND AND REACH
FOR WHAT IS AHEAD.

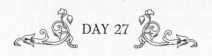

THE GREAT COVER-UP
(PART ONE)

*A man of many friends comes to ruin, but there is
a friend who sticks closer than a brother.*

PROVERBS 18:24

*N*othing is as easy as talking; nothing is as difficult as communicating. Good communication is a longed-for luxury in all kinds of relationships, but it is especially essential in families. And one of the most basic requirements for good communication—*transparency*—is hinted at in the Scripture above.

Before the Fall, Adam and Eve were the picture of true transparency. Not only were they uncovered physically, but they also had nothing to hide emotionally. But after the Fall, "The eyes of both of them were opened, and they knew that they were naked; and they sewed fig leaves together and made themselves loin coverings" (Gen. 3:7).

This is the beginning of "The Great Cover-Up." Many people diligently continue the practice to this day. They spend a great deal of time and energy acquiring façades and veneers in order to hide their insecurities and fears.

Transparency can be very threatening, especially for men. For example, many men believe that to be so vulnerable that they shed tears openly is a sign of weakness. They have been taught that men are to be strong, self-contained and invincible. Fortunately, this pattern has been changing in recent years.

Paul modeled transparency when he wrote to the Corinthians, "For out of much affliction and anguish of heart I wrote to you with many tears; not that you should be made sorrowful, but that you might know the love which I have especially for you" (2 Cor. 2:4). Jesus wept over the death of His friend Lazarus (see John 11:35) and lamented His rejection by hard-hearted Jerusalem (see Luke 13:34).

Reversing "The Great Cover-Up" and becoming open and dropping your guard with others can be risky. It requires a high level of trust and the willingness to accept the other person no matter what his or her transparency reveals. But the rewards of transparency make it worth the risk. True intimacy is enjoyed only by those who are willing to be seen as they really are.

Discuss: Why does being transparent involve risks? On a scale of 1 to 5, with 1 at the top, how would you rate the level of transparency in your family? When have you been the most transparent in your marriage?

Pray: Ask God to enable you to be transparent with Him. Pray that a deeper level of this openness can be incorporated in your marriage and family.

THE REWARDS OF
TRANSPARENCY MAKE
IT WORTH THE RISK.

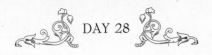
THE GREAT COVER-UP
(PART TWO)

*For now we see in a mirror dimly, but then
face to face; now I know in part, but then I shall know
fully just as I also have been fully known.*

1 CORINTHIANS 13:12

This passage shows that the ultimate level of communication, in which we know fully as we are known, is reserved for heaven. But by God's grace, we can begin to reverse "The Great Cover-Up" even in this life—by growing in our ability to be vulnerable, open and transparent with those we love.

Like most skills, you have to start at the bottom and work up to transparency. Author John Powell described this process in his excellent book *Why Am I Afraid to Tell You Who I Am?* He observed five stages or levels of communication.[1]

Most people start at level five—sharing mere *clichés*. We might call this elevator talk, in which you speak but share nothing: "Hello, how are you?" and "Have a nice day."

Moving up to the fourth level involves sharing *facts*. You are willing to report what you know or what so-and-so said, but you share nothing of yourself.

At level three, people reveal *opinions*—their ideas, judgments and viewpoints. At this level you finally start to come out of your shell and reveal a little of who you are. You risk disagreement or even rejection, so you are very careful at this stage, ready to retreat.

You begin to share *emotions* at level two. Now you are definitely coming out in the open and letting the other person know just what you are feeling. Again, this is risky business and you must be careful not to hurt each other, but it is an essential step if families are to live beyond superficiality.

Level one is *transparency*—being completely open with another, sharing the real you, from the heart. Of course this level of communication requires a large amount of trust and commitment. When you reach the transparency level, you can begin to know even as you are known.

Discuss: Compare how you rated your family's level of communication in the last devotional with the five stages described here. Discuss how you can move toward deeper, more meaningful communication.

Pray: As you pray, think of how intimately God knows you. Ask Him to help your family members grow in their abilities really to know and accept each other.

Note

1. John Powell, *Why Am I Afraid to Tell You Who I Am?* (Allen, Texas: Thomas More Publishing, 1995), n.p.

KEEPING A CLEAN SLATE

Let all bitterness and wrath and anger and clamor and
slander be put away from you, along with all malice.

EPHESIANS 4:31

At one of our conferences, a man boasted to me, "You know, I've been married for 24 years and I've never once apologized to my wife for anything I've done wrong."

"Oh, really?" I said, with a tone that urged him to tell me more.

"Yeah," he said with obvious pride. "Every time we get into a squabble or any kind of disagreement, I just tell her, 'I'm sorry you're mad at me.' I don't admit anything—I just tell her it's too bad she had to get so mad." Then, with a cheesy grin, he admitted, "And all these years she's never realized that I have never once apologized."

It's amazing how many people behave like children trying to weasel out of punishment after getting caught with their hands in the cookie jar. Yet the Scripture is clear: A failure to seek forgiveness and to forgive results in an angry heart, resentment and bitterness. Left to run their unrestrained courses, these emotions will destroy a relationship.

In Ephesians, Paul tells us to put away bitterness and wrath, but he doesn't leave it there; he tells us how. Look at verse 32: "And be kind to one another, tender-hearted, forgiving each other."

Forgiveness makes long-term relationships possible. It keeps our slates clean.

As difficult as it is to ask for forgiveness, it's equally hard to grant it when you have been wronged. You can tell if you have forgiven your mate by asking yourself one question: *Have I given up my desire to punish my mate?* When you let that desire go, you free your spouse and yourself from the bonds of your anger.

It's liberating to admit you're wrong. It's even more liberating when the other person forgives and says, "That's okay—everybody makes mistakes."

Discuss: Why can it be so difficult to admit we're wrong? Take a moment to ask yourself if you need to apologize to your mate about a specific incident.

Pray: Ask for both the courage to admit when you are wrong and the grace to extend forgiveness when you are wronged.

MARRIAGE CEMENT

I want them to be strengthened and joined together with love so that they may be rich in their understanding.

COLOSSIANS 2:2 (NCV)

True partnerships are cemented—"joined together" in Paul's terms—as couples frequently and specifically verbalize their needs for each other. But at some point, between the walk down the wedding aisle and the fifth anniversary, a thief often makes off with our mutual admission of interdependence. Isn't it ironic that marriage, the ultimate declaration of one person's dependence on another, so often winds up being an accomplice to the thief?

Think back to those early days of romance and intrigue. You needed each other then, and you still do. You need her for a balanced and truthful view of yourself. You need him for a full-color view of life, since he looks at life through a different set of lenses.

Often during marriage you begin looking at your differences as hindrances rather than benefits. You are a broader person because of these differences. Why try to change your mate when you *need* these differences?

You need her to believe in you when others don't and you can't. She is your mirror of positive acceptance, expectancy, praise and the belief that you are as significant as ever, though perhaps in different ways. You need him to multiply your laughter, share your tears and add his experience with God to yours.

You need each other to raise healthy and balanced children. Two people tempering one another's weaknesses complement each other's blind spots and help accentuate one another's strong points as they raise children together.

Beware of living independently of one another. Sometimes busy people build their lives around activities only to find, years later, that they are alone. Imprisoned by selfishness and a failure to take risks, they live independently of the person God has sovereignly given them to share life with. You really do need your mate.

Discuss: Make a list of 5 to 10 specific ways you need your mate. Use your list to compose a letter to him or her, expressing your needs. Or take a long walk and talk over the list together.

Pray: Ask that God's Spirit will keep the two of you cemented together, expressing and fulfilling mutual needs.

THINK BACK TO
THOSE EARLY DAYS OF
ROMANCE AND INTRIGUE.
YOU NEEDED EACH
OTHER THEN, AND YOU
STILL DO.

Also Available From
Dennis & Barbara Rainey

Moments Together for Couples
Devotions for Drawing Near to God and One Another
ISBN 978.08307.17545
ISBN 08307.17544

Moments with You
Daily Connections for Couples
ISBN 978.08307.43841
ISBN 08307.43847

Regal
God's Word for Your World™
www.regalbooks.com